YOU ROCK

summersdale

YOU ROCK

An Hachette UK Company
www.hachette.co.uk

Summersdale Publishers Ltd
Part of Octopus Publishing Group Limited
Carmelite House
50 Victoria Embankment
LONDON
EC4Y 0DZ
UK

www.summersdale.com

Printed and bound in the Czech Republic

ISBN: 978-1-78685-256-4

Substantial discounts on bulk quantities of Summersdale books are available to corporations, professional associations and other organisations. For details contact general enquiries: telephone: +44 (0) 1243 771107 or email: enquiries@summersdale.com.

TO....*EV*..................

FROM..*Verity.+*...
     Bella

TO BE BEAUTIFUL
MEANS TO BE
YOURSELF. YOU DON'T
NEED TO BE ACCEPTED
BY OTHERS. YOU NEED
TO ACCEPT YOURSELF.

THÍCH NHẤT HẠNH

NOTHING CAN
DIM THE LIGHT
WHICH SHINES
FROM WITHIN.

MAYA ANGELOU

YOU ARE

AMAZING

BELIEVE YOU CAN
AND YOU'RE
HALFWAY THERE.

THEODORE ROOSEVELT

THE SECRET TO GETTING AHEAD IS GETTING STARTED.

Mark Twain

YOU ARE SO STRONG

YOU'RE PERFECT
WHEN YOU'RE
COMFORTABLE
BEING YOURSELF.

ANSEL ELGORT

COURAGE IS RESISTANCE TO FEAR, MASTERY OF FEAR – NOT ABSENCE OF FEAR.

Mark Twain

THE MORE YOU PRAISE AND CELEBRATE YOUR LIFE, THE MORE THERE IS IN LIFE TO CELEBRATE.

OPRAH WINFREY

TAKE EVERY CHANCE YOU GET

I DON'T WANT OTHER
PEOPLE TO DECIDE
WHO I AM. I WANT
TO DECIDE THAT
FOR MYSELF.

EMMA WATSON

IF MY MIND CAN
CONCEIVE IT,
AND MY HEART
CAN BELIEVE IT —
THEN I CAN
ACHIEVE IT.

JESSE JACKSON

A GOOD HEAD
AND A GOOD HEART
ARE ALWAYS A
FORMIDABLE
COMBINATION.

NELSON
MANDELA

BE YOURSELF.
THE WORLD
WORSHIPS THE
ORIGINAL.

INGRID BERGMAN

DO WHAT

MAKES

YOU HAPPY

COURAGE IS RIGHTLY ESTEEMED THE FIRST OF HUMAN QUALITIES, BECAUSE... IT IS THE QUALITY WHICH GUARANTEES ALL OTHERS.

Winston Churchill

SET YOUR GOALS
HIGH, AND DON'T
STOP TILL YOU
GET THERE.

BO JACKSON

YOUR TIME IS LIMITED, SO DON'T WASTE IT LIVING SOMEONE ELSE'S LIFE.

STEVE JOBS

DON'T WORRY, JUST GO FOR IT!

I PROMISE YOU
THAT EACH AND
EVERY ONE OF YOU
IS MADE TO BE
WHO YOU ARE.

SELENA GOMEZ

ONE CAN NEVER CONSENT TO CREEP <u>WHEN ONE FEELS AN IMPULSE TO SOAR.</u>

HELEN KELLER

EVERY DAY BRINGS
NEW CHOICES.

MARTHA BECK

FOLLOW YOUR PASSION, FOLLOW YOUR HEART, AND THE THINGS YOU NEED WILL COME.

Elizabeth Taylor

BE YOURSELF;
EVERYONE ELSE IS
ALREADY TAKEN.

OSCAR WILDE

YOU WERE BORN TO SHINE!

LIFE SHRINKS
OR EXPANDS
IN PROPORTION
TO ONE'S
COURAGE.

ANAÏS NIN

THE MOST EFFECTIVE WAY TO DO IT, IS TO DO IT.

AMELIA EARHART

FIND OUT WHO YOU ARE
AND BE THAT PERSON...
FIND THAT TRUTH,
LIVE THAT TRUTH
AND EVERYTHING
ELSE WILL COME.

ELLEN
DeGENERES

DO IT

YOUR

WAY

THE ROUGHEST
ROADS OFTEN
LEAD TO THE TOP.

CHRISTINA AGUILERA

IF YOU HAVE AN IDEA, YOU HAVE TO BELIEVE IN YOURSELF WHEN NO ONE ELSE WILL.

Sarah Michelle Gellar

STAY STRONG AND
BE YOURSELF!
IT'S THE BEST
THING YOU
CAN BE.

CARA DELEVINGNE

BE A VOICE, NOT AN ECHO

IF YOU THINK YOU'RE
TOO SMALL TO MAKE
A DIFFERENCE, TRY
SLEEPING WITH
A MOSQUITO.

DALAI LAMA

ONE FINDS
LIMITS BY
PUSHING
THEM.

HERBERT SIMON

IT TAKES
COURAGE TO
GROW UP
AND BECOME
WHO YOU
REALLY ARE.

E. E. CUMMINGS

BE HAPPY

BE TRUE

BE YOU

WE ARE ALL
DIFFERENT.
DON'T JUDGE,
UNDERSTAND
INSTEAD.

ROY T. BENNETT

ALWAYS BE A FIRST-
RATE VERSION OF
YOURSELF AND
NOT A SECOND-
RATE VERSION OF
SOMEONE ELSE.

JUDY GARLAND

NEVER DULL YOUR SHINE FOR SOMEBODY ELSE.

TYRA BANKS

WE WERE SCARED, BUT OUR FEAR WAS NOT AS STRONG AS OUR COURAGE.

Malala Yousafzai

YOU ARE CAPABLE OF AMAZING THINGS

IT IS NOT
THE MOUNTAIN
WE CONQUER
BUT OURSELVES.

EDMUND
HILLARY

YOU ARE NEVER
TOO OLD TO
SET ANOTHER GOAL
OR TO DREAM A
NEW DREAM.

LES BROWN

EACH ONE
OF US CAN MAKE
A DIFFERENCE.
TOGETHER WE
MAKE CHANGE.

BARBARA MIKULSKI

CREATE

THE LIFE

THAT YOU

WANT

TO LIVE

DIFFERENT IS GOOD.
SO DON'T FIT IN,
DON'T SIT STILL,
DON'T EVER TRY
TO BE LESS THAN
WHAT YOU ARE.

ANGELINA JOLIE

IF YOU TRULY POUR
YOUR HEART INTO
WHAT YOU BELIEVE
IN... AMAZING THINGS
CAN AND WILL
HAPPEN.

EMMA WATSON

THE FORMULA OF HAPPINESS AND SUCCESS IS JUST, BEING ACTUALLY YOURSELF, IN THE MOST VIVID POSSIBLE WAY YOU CAN.

MERYL STREEP

YOU ARE THE HERO OF YOUR STORY

LIFE BEGINS AT THE END OF YOUR COMFORT ZONE.

NEALE DONALD WALSCH

THERE ARE MULTIPLE
SIDES TO ALL OF US.
WHO WE ARE - AND
WHO WE MIGHT BE
IF WE FOLLOW
OUR DREAMS.

MILEY CYRUS

THE SCARIEST
MOMENT IS ALWAYS
JUST BEFORE
YOU START.

STEPHEN KING

THERE ARE SO MANY GREAT THINGS IN LIFE: WHY DWELL ON NEGATIVITY?

ZENDAYA

NEVER

APOLOGISE

FOR

BEING

YOURSELF

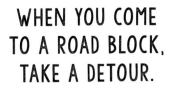

WHEN YOU COME
TO A ROAD BLOCK,
TAKE A DETOUR.

MARY KAY ASH

LIVE AS IF YOU
WERE TO DIE
TOMORROW.
LEARN AS IF YOU
WERE TO LIVE
FOREVER.

ANONYMOUS

YOU MUST DO
THE THING
YOU THINK YOU
CANNOT DO.

ELEANOR ROOSEVELT

DON'T BE AFRAID TO BE BOLD

WE ALL KEEP
DREAMING,
AND LUCKILY,
DREAMS
COME TRUE.

KATIE HOLMES

IT'S NEVER TOO LATE TO TAKE A LEAP OF FAITH AND SEE WHAT WILL HAPPEN – AND TO BE BRAVE IN LIFE.

Jane Fonda

IF THERE IS
NO STRUGGLE,
THERE IS
NO PROGRESS.

FREDERIK DOUGLASS

YOU ARE

ONE OF

A KIND

OVERCOME THE NOTION
THAT WE MUST BE
REGULAR... IT ROBS YOU
OF THE CHANCE TO BE
EXTRAORDINARY.

UTA HAGEN

THERE ARE
NO REGRETS IN LIFE.
JUST LESSONS.

ANONYMOUS

ADVENTURE IS
WORTHWHILE
IN ITSELF.

AMELIA EARHART

RISE

TO THE

CHALLENGE!

LIFE IS VERY INTERESTING... IN THE END, SOME OF YOUR GREATEST PAINS, BECOME YOUR GREATEST STRENGTHS.

DREW BARRYMORE

BE YOURSELF.
BELIEVE IN
WHAT YOU KNOW
AND NOT WHAT
OTHERS SAY
ABOUT YOU.

HAILEE STEINFELD

THE FINAL
FORMING OF A
PERSON'S CHARACTER
LIES IN THEIR
OWN HANDS.

ANNE FRANK

YOU HAVE TO RELY ON
WHATEVER SPARKS
YOU HAVE INSIDE.

LISA KLEYPAS

THERE IS ONLY ONE YOU, SO BE YOU!

TRY NOT TO BECOME A MAN OF SUCCESS, BUT RATHER TRY TO BECOME A MAN OF VALUE.

Albert Einstein

WE MUST
ACCEPT FINITE
DISAPPOINTMENT,
BUT NEVER LOSE
INFINITE HOPE.

MARTIN LUTHER
KING JR

OUR GREATEST
GLORY IS NOT IN
NEVER FALLING, BUT
IN RISING EVERY
TIME WE FALL.

OLIVER GOLDSMITH

COURAGE
WILL TAKE
YOU TO
ALL SORTS
OF PLACES

SELF-TRUST IS THE FIRST SECRET OF SUCCESS.

RALPH WALDO EMERSON

BEAUTY IS NOT
IN THE FACE;
BEAUTY IS A LIGHT
IN THE HEART.

KAHLIL GIBRAN

THE QUESTION ISN'T WHO'S GOING TO LET ME; IT'S WHO'S GOING TO STOP ME.

Ayn Rand

NEVER LOSE

SIGHT OF

WHO YOU ARE

FOLLOW YOUR OWN STAR.

DANTE ALIGHIERI

WHEN LIFE
LOOKS LIKE IT'S
FALLING APART, IT
MAY JUST BE FALLING
INTO PLACE.

BEVERLY SOLOMON

THINK
LITTLE GOALS
AND EXPECT LITTLE
ACHIEVEMENTS.
THINK
BIG GOALS
AND WIN BIG
SUCCESS.

DAVID JOSEPH SCHWARTZ

YOU GOT THIS

IF YOU HAVE SOMETHING YOU'RE REALLY PASSIONATE ABOUT, <u>DON'T LET ANYONE TELL YOU THAT YOU CAN'T DO IT.</u>

SELENA GOMEZ

BE YOURSELF.
NO ONE CAN
EVER TELL YOU
YOU'RE DOING
IT WRONG.

JAMES LEO HERLIHY

DON'T WORRY
ABOUT IT.
THE RIGHT THING
WILL COME AT THE
RIGHT TIME.

DANIELLE STEEL

BE FEARLESS

IN THE

PURSUIT OF

YOUR DREAMS

DO A LITTLE
MORE EACH DAY
THAN YOU THINK
YOU CAN.

LOWELL THOMAS

IT WILL NEVER BE PERFECT, BUT PERFECT IS OVERRATED. PERFECT IS BORING.

Tina Fey on life

IF YOU DON'T
LIVE YOUR
LIFE THEN
WHO WILL?

RIHANNA

BE YOUR BEST SELF!

WHEN YOU HAVE CONFIDENCE, YOU CAN HAVE A LOT OF FUN.

JOE NAMATH

WHAT YOU DO TODAY
CAN IMPROVE YOUR
TOMORROWS.

RALPH MARSTON

RIDE THE ENERGY
OF YOUR OWN
UNIQUE SPIRIT.

GABRIELLE ROTH

INDIVIDUALITY OF
EXPRESSION IS THE
BEGINNING AND
END OF ALL ART.

JOHANN WOLFGANG
VON GOETHE

LIVE FOR THE MOMENT

A PERSON
CAN GROW
ONLY AS MUCH
AS HIS HORIZON
ALLOWS.

JOHN POWELL

DON'T SACRIFICE
YOUR OWN WELFARE
FOR THAT
OF ANOTHER,
NO MATTER
HOW GREAT.

ANONYMOUS

WE DON'T CHANGE... WE HELP OTHER PEOPLE TO CHANGE SO THEY CAN SEE MORE KINDS OF BEAUTY.

Pink

YOU CAN
CHANGE THE
WORLD,
ONE DAY
AT A TIME

NEVER BEND
YOUR HEAD.
ALWAYS
HOLD IT HIGH.
LOOK THE WORLD
STRAIGHT IN
THE EYE.

HELEN KELLER

THE FIRST STEP IS YOU HAVE TO SAY THAT YOU CAN.

WILL SMITH

MAN CANNOT
DISCOVER NEW
OCEANS UNLESS HE
HAS THE COURAGE
TO LOSE SIGHT
OF THE SHORE.

ANDRÉ GIDE

LET NOTHING

STAND IN

YOUR WAY!

DREAMING,
AFTER ALL,
IS A FORM OF
PLANNING.

GLORIA STEINEM

THE BEST WAY
TO PREDICT
THE FUTURE
IS TO
CREATE IT.

ALAN KAY

EMBRACE WHO
YOU ARE.
LITERALLY.
HUG YOURSELF.
ACCEPT WHO
YOU ARE.

ELLEN DeGENERES

SHOW THE WORLD

WORLD

WHAT YOU'RE

MADE OF!

FOLLOW YOUR
INNER MOONLIGHT;
DON'T HIDE THE
MADNESS.

ALLEN GINSBERG

IF YOU'RE PRESENTING YOURSELF WITH CONFIDENCE, YOU CAN PULL OFF PRETTY MUCH ANYTHING.

Katy Perry

WE DON'T KNOW
WHO WE ARE
UNTIL WE
SEE WHAT
WE CAN DO.

MARTHA GRIMES

NO ONE ELSE CAN DO WHAT YOU CAN

LOVE YOURSELF
FIRST AND
EVERYTHING
ELSE FALLS
INTO LINE.

LUCILLE BALL

PROBLEMS ARE GUIDELINES, NOT STOP SIGNS!

ROBERT H. SCHULLER

THIS ABOVE ALL:
TO THINE
OWN SELF
BE TRUE.

WILLIAM SHAKESPEARE

HOLD
YOUR
HEAD
HIGH!

EVERYONE'S DREAM
CAN COME TRUE
IF YOU JUST
STICK TO IT AND
WORK HARD.

SERENA WILLIAMS

NEVER GIVE IN –
NEVER, NEVER, NEVER.

WINSTON CHURCHILL

I DON'T THINK LIMITS.

USAIN BOLT

DREAM BIG

SET GOALS

TAKE ACTION

WE LEARN FROM FAILURE, NOT FROM SUCCESS!

BRAM STOKER

YOU DON'T NEED ANYBODY
TO TELL YOU WHO YOU ARE
OR WHAT YOU ARE.
YOU ARE WHAT
YOU ARE.

JOHN LENNON

SUCCESS IS THE SUM OF SMALL EFFORTS REPEATED DAY IN AND DAY OUT.

Robert J. Collier

TRUST YOUR
INSTINCTS;
YOU KNOW
WHAT TO DO

LIFE ISN'T
ABOUT WAITING
FOR THE STORM
TO PASS.
IT'S ABOUT
LEARNING TO
DANCE IN THE RAIN.

VIVIAN GREENE

THE IMPORTANT THING IS NOT TO STOP QUESTIONING.

ALBERT EINSTEIN

A BIRD DOESN'T SING
BECAUSE HE HAS AN
ANSWER. HE SINGS
BECAUSE HE HAS
A SONG.

JOAN WALSH ANGLUND

YOU
ARE AN
ACHIEVER

FIND OUT
WHO YOU ARE
AND DO IT
ON PURPOSE.

DOLLY PARTON

BEAUTY IS BEING THE BEST POSSIBLE VERSION OF YOURSELF.

Audrey Hepburn

A SMILE IS
A CURVE
THAT SETS
EVERYTHING
STRAIGHT.

PHYLLIS DILLER

COURAGE
IS FOUND
IN UNLIKELY
PLACES.

J. R. R. TOLKIEN

IF YOU BELIEVE
IN YOURSELF,
EVERYONE
ELSE WILL TOO

MOTIVATION IS WHEN YOUR DREAMS PUT ON WORK CLOTHES.

BENJAMIN FRANKLIN

EACH TIME WE FACE
OUR FEAR, WE GAIN
STRENGTH, COURAGE
AND CONFIDENCE
IN THE DOING.

THEODORE ROOSEVELT

EVERY SMALL
POSITIVE CHANGE
WE CAN MAKE IN
OURSELVES REPAYS
US IN CONFIDENCE
IN THE FUTURE.

ALICE WALKER

I FINALLY FIGURED
OUT THE ONLY
REASON TO BE ALIVE
IS TO ENJOY IT.

RITA MAE BROWN

THE POWER TO
SUCCEED IS
WITHIN YOU

I CAN, THEREFORE I AM.

SIMONE WEIL

YOUR SUCCESS
WILL BE DETERMINED
BY YOUR OWN
CONFIDENCE.

MICHELLE OBAMA

I'M A BIG BELIEVER
IN ACCEPTING
YOURSELF AND NOT
REALLY WORRYING
ABOUT IT.

JENNIFER LAWRENCE

IT'S ALWAYS TOO SOON TO QUIT.

NORMAN VINCENT PEALE

GO OUT THERE AND GET IT!

LISTEN TO
YOUR HEART
ABOVE ALL
OTHER VOICES.

MARTA KAGAN

THERE IS NOTHING BETTER THAN ACHIEVING YOUR GOALS, WHATEVER THEY MIGHT BE.

Paloma Faith

IF YOU WAIT FOR
THINGS TO BE PERFECT
YOU'LL JUST MISS
OUT ON LIFE.

CHRIS PRATT

A SHIP IS SAFE
IN HARBOUR,
BUT THAT IS <u>NOT</u>
<u>WHAT SHIPS ARE</u>
<u>BUILT FOR.</u>

JOHN A. SHEDD

BE BRAVE.
TAKE RISKS.
NOTHING CAN
SUBSTITUTE
EXPERIENCE.

PAULO COELHO

PUT

YOURSELF

FORWARD

NEVER GIVE UP!
FAILURE AND
REJECTION ARE ONLY
THE FIRST STEP
TO SUCCEEDING.

JIM VALVANO

TO BE YOURSELF
IN A WORLD THAT
IS CONSTANTLY
TRYING TO MAKE YOU
SOMETHING ELSE
IS THE GREATEST
ACCOMPLISHMENT.

RALPH WALDO EMERSON

OPTIMISM IS THE FAITH THAT LEADS TO ACHIEVEMENT.

Helen Keller

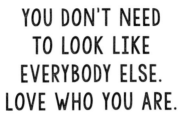

YOU DON'T NEED
TO LOOK LIKE
EVERYBODY ELSE.
LOVE WHO YOU ARE.

LEA MICHELE

NOTHING IS
IMPOSSIBLE. THE
WORD ITSELF SAYS
'I'M POSSIBLE!'

AUDREY HEPBURN

YOU
ROCK!

If you're interested in finding out more about our books, find us on Facebook at SUMMERSDALE PUBLISHERS and follow us on Twitter at @SUMMERSDALE.

WWW.SUMMERSDALE.COM

YOU

ROCK!

If you're interested in finding out more about our books, find us on Facebook at SUMMERSDALE PUBLISHERS and follow us on Twitter at @SUMMERSDALE.

WWW.SUMMERSDALE.COM